D0547063

Life is a Choice

A Guide to Success in Life

Dr. David Washington

WASHINGTON & CO.

EDUCATE • ENCOURAGE • ENTERTAIN

Raleigh, North Carolina

Published by
Washington & Company, LLC

Washington & Company
410 N. Boylan Avenue
Raleigh, North Carolina, 27603

Printed in the United States of America
10 9 8 7 6 5 4 3 2 1

Library of Congress Control Number: 2011941018

ISBN: 978-0-615-55220-0

Associate Editor: Laura C. Bethea
Associate Editor: Melisa Kriz

This book is dedicated to every person that plays
the game of life to the fullest.

Acknowledgments

I would like to thank God for all of His immaculate blessings in my life.

I would like to thank the people who contributed to my successes in life:

My wife, Thu Washington, who greatly contributed to my success with her constant support and devotion. I am extremely grateful to have such a wonderful friend, confidant, and companion. Thank you, Babe—I love you.

To my three wonderful children, David, Sean, and Jade— Daddy loves you.

To my mother, Clementine Washington. When I was younger, my mother worked long hours and tolerated unbearable working conditions for my older brother and me. Thank you, Mom—I love you.

To all of my friends and mentors, too numerous to mention. Thank you to all of you. I truly appreciate every one of you.

I would like also to thank the faculty and staff of Central Texas College, Excelsior College, Central Michigan University, Webster University, and North Carolina State University for the educational opportunities.

.

Contents

Contents

The Battle

It is not the external battle that we must fight and win. There is a more important and greater battle, the battle within. Self-doubt, disbelief, and criticism our enemy employs, but self confidence, belief, and affirmation are the weapons that we must forge. This opponent is strong and persuasive in his way, but we must be stronger and smarter to make it through each day. The battle that we fight is a constant, this is true, but this is the fight worth having, the battle within you. We must persist in this battle, for there is no cavalry here. We must continue, for we are so near. Near to the victory, near to the triumph, near to our destined end. We are near to our desires, but first we must fight the most important battle... The battle within.

- Dr. David Washington

Introduction

"A journey of a thousand miles begins with a single step."

-Lao Tzu
Chinese Philosopher

To God be the glory. I have been fortunate enough with my life that I've been able to achieve something out of nothing, and I give God the glory for everything that He has done with my life. I know if you are in the secular world you may not understand the above statement, but I'm not saying that this book is not for you. I'm just telling you what I know for me, and for each person, it is a little bit different. My faith has helped me to overcome the obstacles I have faced. I have been fortunate enough that in addition to my faith, I learned some key lessons and heeded the wisdom of those lessons.

I have gone through hard parts, rough patches, heartache, and misery, but I have been able to achieve greatness and a real level of success. My dear friend, I am sharing with you what has taken me years to obtain and I hope that you take this information to heart and make it your own. Whatever you learn from this book, I hope it inspires your life, impacts you in a real way, and clicks something in your mind to say, "I can make it happen too."

It does not matter if you are a kid in the suburbs or a kid in the projects, a CEO of a Fortune 500 company, or a CEO of a start-up in your garage, these lessons apply to everyone. Women, men, black, white, Jew, Gentile,—we all feel pain, we all go through hard times, and we are all looking for ways to improve our lives.

In this book, I will explain in a simple-to-understand manner, how to obtain success in life—no lofty theories. This book is written in a conversational and direct manner to help you understand each concept. I want you to understand that success in life is obtainable. It is not going to be easy, but with a plan, it can be achieved. I hope that you will be inspired by the message and look at this book as your personal advisor.

I hope something that is in this book triggers something in your heart so that you can go forward and do great things. Please let me know if you have made a breakthrough or a success, as I would love to hear how you are doing. The teacher in me enjoys seeing my students succeed. With this book, you can be one of my students, and I can learn from you as well. I want to hear your stories and triumphs, so please email me at david@washingtonandco.com.

Ladies and gentlemen, may this book be a blessing to you, and I hope to plant a seed to help you reach your full potential in life. I wish you the very best, and God bless.

Be empowered.

Chapter 1:

Don't Let Fear Conquer You

"Don't fall victim to what I call the 'ready-aim-aim-aim-aim syndrome.' You must be willing to fire."

-George S. Patton
U.S. Army General

A lot of times, people do not understand that I am scared to death when I'm doing some of this stuff, between running a business, completing my PhD, or changing my life. I did not know how any of these endeavors were going to work out. I would be telling a boldface lie if I said I did not question the outcome. However, I came to grips with this: whatever is going to happen is going to happen regardless, so do your very best and leave the fear behind.

Fear has a paralyzing effect. It will stop you in midstream or stop you from applying for that business loan or the job you truly desire. It will stop you from talking to the person across the room who might be your soul mate. It will prevent you from enjoying the best and most beautiful things about life. Because you're scared, you stop. Because you're scared, you freeze. You were not born with that spirit of fear; you learned it. Someone may have said to you:

"You can't do that."

"That's not possible."

"That's outside of the realm of possibilities for you."

"That's not your life."

You may have started to believe what they have said, but you must shake off the fear. It is only going to hinder and cripple you. It's keeping you from asking for that promotion on your job. It is keeping you from asking for that new opportunity that you have worked hard for and are rightfully entitled to.

You may fear the word "no." "No" is a natural process to "yes." You're going to hear "no" a lot; I've heard it a few times.

"No, we're not interested."

"No, we don't want it."

"No, you can't have this."

That's perfectly fine, because for every "no," there is somebody else out there that will say "yes." You just have not gotten to them yet. You have to get through these "no's" to get to that "yes." You have to get pass the people who don't want what you are offering and get to the person that does.

For example, when I was pursuing my PhD, I received a number of rejection letters: they said that I was not properly prepared or did not have the right standardized test scores. However, I kept going and continued to apply to universities. My feelings were hurt, but I stomached the pain and continued to apply.

I knew that I could succeed in a PhD

program. My belief was rooted in the fact that I was not afraid of failure. I was not scared of the work or regimen of study, because I knew that if I gave my best efforts, I would be victorious. Through sheer determination and hard work, my

opportunity came; not only was I accepted into a PhD program, but I was accepted into a Tier One University. A Tier One University is recognized as the highest level of educational institution. Later, I went on to set a departmental record for the fastest graduation time. On average, it takes four to seven years to complete a PhD. I completed my PhD, including my dissertation, in three years.

This would not have been possible if I had not overcome my fear of rejection. When you leave the fear behind you can achieve amazing outcomes, and many people who doubted my abilities had to pay respect to my accomplishments.

Now when I hear "no," I thank the person for his time and move forward. I know that in the time I'm talking with a "no person," I could be talking to a person who might be my "yes."

When I get rejected, I ask, "Why?" If someone tells you that you're not what he is looking for, ask, "I don't mean to intrude, but could you please tell me why? I want to make sure that this doesn't hinder me in the future." The moment of courage you exhibit in asking "why" may open up a world of opportunity. If you don't know the reason, you don't know what to fix.

In business, we often talk about the fact that half of marketing budgets are wasted. The reason is that we do not ask why.

"Why did this not work out?"

"Why did you not like this?"

"Tell me what I can do to improve this."

You have paid the price of admission. You have gone through the rejection, so why shouldn't you know why? If someone gives you an answer, make the adjustments as needed and move forward. That's the process of learning.

Your behavior changes as you learn, but you've got to get over the fear. Stop giving yourself negative messages:

"They're not going to like me."

"They're not going to give me what I need."

"They're not going to see me as valuable."

Start saying to yourself:

"They are going to see me as valuable."

"I am worthwhile."

"If this person doesn't see my value, someone else will."

There are over six billion people on this planet. If you are selling a product or a service, trying to improve a world problem, or trying to achieve something, out of six billion people, there has got to be at least one person who can help.

That's what I love about this opportunity we call life. Every day that we awake, we can change our path, but we need the courage to do so. Dear friend, have courage, because courage will carry you a long way.

Lesson 1:
Avoiding Procrastination

Procrastination is the source of inaction and failure. The tips below will help you if you have a problem with procrastination.

Break the task into smaller parts.

One reason for procrastination is fear of the size of the work. If the work is broken down into smaller, manageable pieces, the task will not seem overwhelming.

Work from a short, prioritized list.

How many times have you started your day with a long list of tasks to complete only to find that at the end of your day, you removed only two items? This hurts your motivation and makes you feel like you have gotten farther behind. Use a short, prioritized list. You will move faster through the list, and if you do not complete everything on it, the most important items are completed.

Celebrate small victories and milestones.

It is important to keep your morale up when working on a difficult task. When you hit a milestone, take the time to celebrate the event. If it is no more than taking yourself to a movie, do it. Take a rest, and then get back to work.

Track progress.

Chart the progress of your work. A visual representation will help you stay motivated and serve as a map to where you are in the work.

Generally, procrastination is based upon fear, and it is the enemy of success. Do not let procrastination take hold in your habits; once procrastination becomes a habit, it is hard to break. Be empowered.

Chapter 2:

Attitude is the Ultimate Key

"Man can alter his life by altering his thinking."

-James Williams
American Psychologist

Your attitude is your perspective on life and how you view the world. If a person has a negative attitude about life, only negative things will manifest. Many individuals do not understand why life is difficult for them, but their difficulties can be linked to their attitude. Think for a moment; if your internal dialogue sounds like the following, how successful do you think you will be?

"I can't make it."

"This is going to be impossible."

"There is no way I can win."

What we say to ourselves is what we become. Our mind and soul are where our most important actions come from, and if the attitude is negative, the actions will be negative.

My most enlightening setback that helped me understand the power of attitude occurred when I was fourteen years old. My mother lost her low-wage job. When she informed me, I immediately knew the implications. We could easily be evicted from our modest home. I went to the bedroom that my mother, my brother, and I shared, fell on the bed, and looked up at the rain-stained ceiling. I pondered how long it would take for us to lose our home and how long before the utility workers turned off the power. A spirit rose inside of me and said, "Get up, it is not over yet." I give God the credit for that spirit to help me face the insurmountable. I rose from that bed determined, renewed, and ready to face the task at hand.

I recognized that my attitude and actions would dictate failure or success, so I maintained a positive attitude and started thinking of alternatives to solve problems. I said to myself, "I'm going to beat this. I can do something about my situation." By uttering those words, I gained strength, confidence, and power. I had to keep saying those words, but each time I did, I was stronger in heart and will. Had I taken a defeatist position, I would have been defeated by my circumstances. Once my attitude took hold, everything else started to change. I did not see the problems; I started seeing the possibilities. I started believing that I was going to make it. My attitude gave me the courage to pursue employment at age fourteen.

I was tall for my age and could pass as an older teenager. I worked hard on my jobs, because I knew what was at stake, and I maintained a positive attitude, which made the work easier. By my senior year of high school, I was working four jobs, attending school, and managing the major responsibilities of the household. My attitude sustained me in those conditions and allowed me to recognize how truly blessed I am.

I worked at a grocery store in the floral department, which was in the front of the store. Each day, I greeted every person that passed my department with a big smile and the question, "Good day. How are you?" When the person said, "Fine, how are you?" I replied, "I'm doing fantastic." This dialogue puzzled some of my customers, because in some cases, the person had seen me working in another store earlier that day and might wonder how I could be "doing fantastic." I recognized a simple truth: I was fantastic because I chose to be.

We are granted free will to choose our disposition in life. We can determine our perspective of the world around us. I recognized that there were people in this world suffering more than myself. I struggled working all of those jobs, but a child in intensive care from the moment of birth that will require care for the rest of his life may never know the experiences of work or play. Although my father abandoned me, there was a child who would have been glad her father was not in the household, because she did not know what was in store for her when she arrived home. I was raised in poverty, but someone had to climb into a dumpster in the hope of finding a scrap of food. I was doing fantastic because I had control of my limbs, I was working to change my situation, I was doing something about my life, and I had a lot to be thankful for. I was grateful for being able to work all of those jobs, as they were opportunities, not shackles. If you have the wrong attitude, you will take the wrong position, and before long, your life will reflect a poor attitude. With the proper attitude, life opens itself up.

Because my attitude was always positive about what I was doing, even when things were not going my way, opportunities came forward that previously would not have been available.

Your mental state is more important than your physical circumstances. Change your attitude, and you will change your outcomes.

Lesson 2:
How to Improve Attitude

Our attitude will be the key component to assist us in reaching success in life. Below are some tips to help you improve your attitude.

Clean your environment.

The environment surrounding you has an effect on your attitude. When you clean up your surroundings, it gives you a sense of control and helps you to see clearly. When clutter is removed, you can see what you are working with, and the physical activity and work of cleaning helps you to relieve stress.

Think about the good things in your life.

Too often, we think about what we do not have. I encourage you to think about what you do have and be thankful for those things. When I am down, I switch my attitude by thinking of the good things in my life; I start with the basics and work my way up. Thoughts of positive attributes eliminate a negative attitude.

Use music and books.

I like to read and hear something positive each morning. During the course of the day, I play jazz and upbeat music to facilitate a good mood in my office. Listening to uplifting music can help you shake off a bad attitude.

Focus on goals, not the problem.

Your attitude can take a nose dive when you focus purely on the problem. Problems are constant in life; this is why it is important to focus on the goal. In the midst of a problem, recognize that your problem is temporary and will pass. Your attitude and mood will improve when you start working on a solution that will get you to your goal.

Make plans for the future.

Making plans helps create a positive attitude, because it shows that your current reality will not last forever. Making plans requires you to focus and direct your energies toward something other than a bad attitude.

Get out of your space.

If you are feeling bad, go outside or take a short walk around the office. Those moments may be what you need to improve your attitude. Scheduling a time in the day to engage in physical activity helps to release stress and improve your attitude.

Smile.

Smiling helps to improve your attitude, and the act of smiling helps to regulate your thoughts. Sharing a laugh with a friend will help to improve your attitude.

Our attitudes are adjustable, but we must recognize that we have the power to change them. Be empowered.

Chapter 3:

Do It with Passion

"And whatsoever ye do, do it heartily, as to the
Lord, and not unto men."

Colossians 3:23
Holy Bible, King James Version

No matter what you wish to do, do it with
passion. A person with passion has a light that
burns brightly and causes others to be drawn to
this individual. In today's society, it is rare to
find an individual who is truly excited and
engaged about his vocation or life prospects. The
individual with passion stands above the rest
because he is interested, focused, and excited
about his endeavor. Passion drives him to excel
far beyond his peers, because the individual with

passion is working for a different reason. He desires to a make a lasting impression on the world via his work or life's contribution.

The Great Pyramid of Giza is an example of passion. The Great Pyramid has been the subject of much examination and theorizing. The estimate of the workforce ranges from fourteen thousand to fifty thousand. It is estimated the Great Pyramid took ten years to build, and a hundred years total to complete all the constructions of the Giza Plateau. One thing is known: the engineers, architects, and other builders paid great attention to the erection of the Great Pyramid and the other constructions of the Giza Plateau. In an article in *Civil Engineering Magazine,* Dr. Craig Smith says this:

> The logistics of construction at the Giza site are staggering when you think that the ancient Egyptians had no pulleys, no wheels, and no iron tools. Yet, the dimensions of the pyramid are

extremely accurate and the site was leveled within a fraction of an inch over the entire 13.1-acre base. This is comparable to the accuracy possible with modern construction methods and laser leveling. That's astounding. With their 'rudimentary tools,' the pyramid builders of ancient Egypt were about as accurate as we are today with 20th century technology.[1]

You may ask, "Why is this important to achieving success in life?" The answer is passion. The pyramids are still standing because the builders were concerned about the final product. They wanted their work to stand the test of time. The Great Pyramid was built with longevity in mind. There was no detail too small to be addressed, and the Great Pyramid had a security system to prevent robbers from looting the pharaoh's grave. That is passion. The builders understood this principle: do your work with passion. Your deeds, works, or life focus should stand for an eternity.

Success is predicated upon passion, because without passion in your work, success is hard to obtain and maintain. We have all been involved in a project or process that we had no passion for. The task was harder, it took longer and it was easy to quit at the first sign of a problem. However, think about a time when you were fully engaged in a project. Time seemed to fly by; the task may have been difficult, but you did not mind the extra effort. At the end of the process you felt a sense of pride from completing the task. You may be wondering, "How can I be successful working a dead end job? How can I be passionate or engaged about that?" Do not worry; I have an answer and explanation for you.

To become passionate about a "dead-end job," change your perspective. There are no dead-end jobs, just dead-end people. Every job presents an opportunity for advancement; I should know; I have had more than my fair share of minimal skill jobs. I have been a florist, a day laborer, a fast food restaurant worker, a bus-boy, and a video store clerk. I have dug ditches, flipped burgers, mopped floors, and hauled bricks. However, I did all these jobs with passion, which have led to promotion for me. I found passion in my jobs because I wanted my work to say something about me. Although the work was not glamorous, I wanted my work to standout as superior. When I dug a ditch, I wanted the ditch to be the best in the state of Alabama. When I made a floral arrangement, I wanted it to look like it came from the premier florist shop in the city. When I cleared tables at the restaurant, I wanted people to say, "That young man cares about his job and us." My passion not only manifested in my work but also in my dress. My uniforms were pressed and my shoes shined, because I wanted to look like the professional that I was. I wanted every nuance of my work to be a strong representation of me, but that would not be possible without passion.

However, allow me to offer a rationale for why you need passion even when you are not in your dream position or job. Passion will bring you what you seek.

Passion in your work opens the door for people to see what you can be. Every day we audition for the job or position we want. Every day through our work or actions, we make a representation to the world. It is not only the job you hold, but the way you hold the job. I learned this lesson early in life and reaped major benefits from this. In my professional life, I have obtained major acclaim for my work inside of the classroom, which eventually led to me becoming an assistant dean in a Tier One University at age twenty-eight. The reason was passion. I did not wait for someone to tell me what I should do; I saw a problem and took the initiative to fix it. Passion is a differentiating factor that can move an individual forward. Many people do not put the right amount of passion into their given activities; they do not do it with their heart. They are going through the motions and getting go-through-the-motion results. Had they done their work with passion, they would have achieved a better outcome.

Success is about passion, and passion is saying, "I'm going to do this job and do it to the best of my ability." The next time you pick up a job; ask yourself, "Am I doing this with passion?"

End Note:

Smith, Craig. "Program Management B.C." *Civil Engineering Magazine,* June 1999.

Lesson 3:

Finding Passion

Ralph Waldo Emerson wrote, "Nothing great was ever achieved without enthusiasm." Passion is the fuel of success. If you are having problems finding passion in your work, these tips will help you.

Focus your efforts on the end user.

We can become distracted with the hustle and bustle of life and forget the people we are trying to serve. With a lack of focus, we may start seeing our jobs as pointless. Think about why you chose your current profession, and rededicate yourself to that purpose. If you work in a job that is not your purpose, a great way to find passion is to think about the end user of your product or service. Ask, "Would I be happy with this service or product?" You will start to take the work more seriously and attend to your duties with more attention, and this is the start of passion.

Recognize the significance of your role.

Many people have convinced themselves that their jobs are not important, but there is nothing further from the truth. If you make burgers for a living, that has importance, because you are responsible for the food that will be consumed by another human being, and trust me, that is very important. Don't believe me? Think of the *E. coli* problems that Jack in the Box had in the early 1990s. All labor has value, but it is up to you to recognize the value and significance of your work.

Learn something new every day.

Learning begets excitement, which leads to passion. When you learn something new and try out new experiences, it is easy to get excited and energized about the process. This requires you to take initiative on your part, but the benefits are multifold. As you learn more, people ask your opinion, and this provides a nice feeling of significance. Promotion becomes an easier proposition. You develop more confidence and courage to try more things. In essence, learning promotes growth and success in life.

Take on new challenges at work.

When you step up for new challenges, you may have to use skills and knowledge that you have not previously used, and this helps to promote passion. A new challenge will give you the room you need to spread your wings and fly. Volunteering is a great way to get noticed by your superiors. I have acquired wonderful experiences and skills because I volunteered for assignments, and I benefited greatly from those assignments.

Your level of passion will match your level of success. Be empowered.

Chapter 4:

Hard Work:
There Is No Substitute

▍▎▍▎▍

"We all have dreams. But in order to make dreams come into reality, it takes an awful lot of determination, dedication, self-discipline, and effort."

-Jesse Owens
Olympic Gold Medalist

I n our user-friendly, Google apps-clicks society, we may have forgotten the importance of hard work. Some of us run from hard work like a politician running from a news camera after being caught with his celebrity mistress, but do not fear hard work if you want success.

Any person who has achieved success had to work hard. He had to crack out some midnight oil, open the store early, or wait for hours for a key decision maker. He understands that without hard work, the foundation of his success would be tenuous at best. Success solely based on family connections, happenstance, demographic background, beauty, or any other random occurrence is not sustainable. For example, an individual's beauty may open some doors, but at the end of the day, that person is going to need to produce. You may say, "I hear what you are saying, but what about smart people? They don't have to work as hard." Intelligence alone does not achieve success, but do not take my word for it. Let's look at the research of psychologist Dr. Daniel Goleman.

Dr. Goleman is famous for his work on the concept of emotional intelligence. He researched various organizations to find the core to effective leadership. In his investigations, he uncovered technical skills and intellect serve as "threshold capabilities" for success in leadership. In an article published in the *Harvard Business Review,* Dr. Goleman stated the following:

> It's not that IQ and technical skills are irrelevant. They do matter, but mainly as "threshold capabilities"; that is, they are the entry-level requirements for executive positions. But my research, along with other recent studies, clearly shows that emotional intelligence is the sine qua non of leadership. Without it, a person can have the best training in the world, an incisive, analytical mind, and an endless supply of smart ideas, but he still won't make a great leader.[1]

Dr. Goleman's work helps to make a point I would like you to think about. A person can be smart, lazy and fail dramatically, while another person can have minimal intellect yet work like the dickens and be wildly successful. This is not to discount talent or intelligence but to clarify their roles in success. Bill Gates is smart, but he worked hard to build Microsoft. Paul Allen and Bill Gates invested countless hours of hard work to develop the foundation of a young company called Microsoft. Oprah Winfrey is smart, but she worked hard from age nineteen forward to develop a billion dollar media dynasty. Jay-Z is smart, but he worked hard to grow his rap empire. Before he was a headliner, he started in music by banging out drum beats on his mother's kitchen table. Being gifted with natural abilities cannot hurt your chances of reaching success, but those abilities alone will not guarantee success. Ability plus hard work is the winning formula.

Over the years, I heard numerous people complain about their lack of achievement in life. They make statements like these:

"I would do better in life, but it's my boss's fault."

"I could have gone to school, but my kids prevented me from doing it."

"You're just lucky. That's why you made it."

What is missing from their analysis is the measure of effort they have placed into reaching their goals. In most cases, they did not work hard enough to make their dreams reality. Do not let that happen to you.

I have read many books, earned credentials, and achieved much success, but every morning when I wake, I recognize the truth that I am responsible for my success. If I do not put in the necessary work, no one is going to do it for me, and at the end of the day, there is no substitute for hard work. It does not matter how slick, smart, beautiful, cute, kind, aware, politically connected or wealthy you are. Without hard work, success is fleeting. What you put in is what you get out.

End Note:
Goleman, Daniel. "What makes a leader?" *Harvard Business Review,* January 2004, Vol. 82 Issue 1, p. 82-91.

Lesson 4:

Making Work Work for You

Hard work is critical for success, but you don't have to work yourself to death to achieve it. The following tips will help you make the most of your time and effort.

Backward plan your work.

Backward planning means starting the planning process from the end and working backward. This is a dynamic way to plan work, because you have an opportunity to think about the resources, tools, and processes that are needed to complete a project. Close your eyes and visualize the end point, and like watching a movie in rewind, see the process. See deep into the project, and think about large and small details. Once you have completed this process, record what you saw. Place the activities in order as they relate to time and process. Backward planning will help you move forward faster.

Develop an organization system.

Organization is the key to not overworking yourself. Organization is putting together a system by which you categorize, arrange, and manage information. Think about the major activities of your life such as work and family, and then think of the easiest way to manage your important dates, documents, and contacts. Is your cell phone best, or your online calendar? The method of organization is not as important as the usability of the system. The system must be something you can use and sustain. New Year's resolutions fail because people set goals that are unrealistic or unsustainable. Your organization system must be sustainable to work, and it must be accessible to be functional. Periodically purge your system to ensure that your system does not become cluttered, and make sure that you have a back-up system in case of an emergency.

Prepare for each day.

Prepare the night before for a smooth transition into the day. You know the anxiety you feel before Monday? You are anxious because the weekend is concluding, and you do not know what waits for you on Monday. You can relieve some of that anxiety by preparing yourself mentally and physically for Monday. On Sunday evening, say to yourself one of the following phrases: "Monday is going to be a great day," or "I'm looking forward to work tomorrow," or "Tomorrow will be a fantastic day." You will alleviate the anxiety associated with Monday. Once your mind is on board, the rest of the process comes easier. Lay out your clothes, make sure that your work or school materials are packed, and get a good night's rest. With your mind and body ready for the next day, you can achieve more.

Use your time wisely.

At work or school, you may find your attention drifting to surfing the web or social media interactions. A break is okay, but not at the cost of your work. Time is wasted in constantly checking email. Limit how often you check email; you may want to only check every two hours instead of every fifteen minutes. You can get more done with your day, because you have blocks of time instead of pieces.

Hard work does not have to be hard on you, if you coordinate and execute your work. Be empowered.

Chapter 5:

Don't Fall Out

IｌｌｌｌＩ

"Nothing in the world can take the place of Persistence. Talent will not; nothing is more common than unsuccessful men with talent. Genius will not; unrewarded genius is almost a proverb. Education will not; the world is full of educated derelicts. Persistence and determination alone are omnipotent."

-Calvin Coolidge
30th president of US (1872-1933)

In life, we may face levels of adversity that may prompt us to quit, but I encourage you not to give in to this urge. In the U.S. Army, I learned a valuable lesson about emotional endurance. The Armed Services are known for the physical requirements that it places upon soldiers. Popular media emphasizes the physical toughness of the men and women in uniform, and make no mistake, they are physically strong. However, the basis of their strength is not their muscle, but their mind. I learned this lesson on a hot summer day in basic training.

When I entered basic training at Fort Jackson, South Carolina, I must admit that I detested running. I had a motto about running, "Only run when being chased." I started a run fine, but toward the end, I habitually fell out until one day, Drill Sergeant Craig pulled me aside to talk. Allow me to explain the role of the Drill Sergeant. A drill sergeant is a noncommissioned officer who teaches the new recruits basic military operations. He teaches various subjects from military honors and traditions to weapons and tactics, and a core area of instruction is physical fitness. However, I feel the most important area the Drill Sergeant influences is that of mental toughness, and this was made evident to me on a routine run.

The day started like any other. I woke up at "o'dark thirty" and prepared for morning physical training. I went downstairs with my unit, we stretched out, and we were on our way. Toward the end of the run, I fell out, and Drill Sergeant Craig broke ranks and followed me. He said, "Why are you stopping?!" I replied, "I am tired, Drill Sergeant!" Drill Sergeant Craig paused. This was unusual because at this point, he is supposed to do the stereotypical Drill Sergeant yelling, but he used something different; he used the opportunity as a "teachable moment." The teachable moment is the perfect alignment of a set of circumstances that helps to explain for a student a concept. Drill Sergeant Craig said, "Washington, what's going on with you? Do you know you must run twice as hard to catch up versus staying in the run? You're so close to the end, Washington it's not your muscles that are falling out, it's your mind."

In that moment, Drill Sergeant Craig's statement clarified the situation. I was falling out at the point when it was most crucial to push on: toward the end. I was expending more time, more energy, and effort by falling out than by staying in the run. My muscles were strong enough to complete the run, but my mind was not committed to the task. Self-doubt and lack of concentration was all that was needed for me to not complete the run. This incident details an important situation that occurs many times in life.

Many times, we give up when the breakthrough is right around the corner. I have seen this occur many times in the academic environment. As a professor, I saw many students who were close to completing a semester or their degree but "fell out" when it was most crucial to push on. As a student, I have seen many people complete the course requirements for the PhD only to stall on the most important portion, the dissertation. The dissertation is the original research that the student must produce to become a PhD. They said, "I just completed my course work, so I am going to take a break for a few weeks." The break stretches from a few weeks to a month, from a month to a semester, from a semester to two semesters, and from two semesters to two years. The run, in this case the PhD program, was almost over. However, the person did not persist at the most crucial time.

When we fall out, we miss the power of our momentum. We are already warmed up and in motion, and it is easier to stay in motion than restart. Many of my colleagues in the program were extremely smart and well equipped to complete the program, but they missed this principle, and it cost them. In order to complete the program, many of them had to spend more time, more energy, more effort and, in this situation, more money to complete the same degree. Had they "stayed in the run" and not fallen out, they could have completed the program without the additional cost.

You may be wondering, "What happened with the run?" Let me tell you. A few days after

Drill Sergeant Craig talked with me, we had another run. It started as usual; we stretched for physical training and prepared for the run. This time, I was ready not only physically, but mentally. The run started, and we were on our way. When we got to the point where I usually fell out, Drill Sergeant Craig ran to my side and said, "Isn't this where you fall out?!" I fell out alright and ran to the front of the platoon and led them in. When the run was over, he looked at me with admiration in his eyes, smiled and nodded, because I made it. He was right; it was my mind. I have never forgotten the lesson that a good teacher taught me.

I encourage you not to fall out when you are almost there. Persist, because your breakthrough is much closer than you think. Don't fall out! Remember, it is your mind, not your muscles.

Lesson 5:

Don't Fall Out

We often fall out when success is around the corner. The following tips will help you stay in the run.

Maintain a positive attitude.

An attitude is an evaluative statement about a person, place, thing, or event, and it is under your control. You can change your attitude like you change a shirt. Mastering your internal dialogue will be difficult at first, but the more you concentrate on it, the better you will get at mastering your thoughts. Your thoughts become your actions. If you think negatively, negative actions will occur. If you think positively, positive actions will occur. Guard your mind and thoughts like you would guard a room full of money.

Visualize the end.

If you can see it, you can achieve it. Visualization of the end product or result is half of the battle. An unclear or obstructed vision of the end can cause problems in decision making, action, and thoughts. Being clear on the end result helps you to reach your desired destination. Find a quiet place to reflect on the end result. Close your eyes and see the end goal. Be specific. See the end in high-definition quality. Every day, until the goal is realized, visualize the goal. Committing the goal to paper will help in this process.

Surround yourself with people interested in your success.

It is hard to push a boulder uphill, especially when someone is sitting on it. Negative people will make you want to fall out, so remove the negative person from the equation. Negative people are like an infectious disease; if you let them stay around, their negative sentiments will rub off onto you. Positive people help to keep your spirits up when the going gets tough. How do you find these positive people? Observe their actions from a distance. Do they help others or themselves? Ask around: "Who can you count on? Who is sincere in their dealings?" Once you have a list of people, introduce yourself to them and see where the conversation leads you. Important note: do not be a user. A user is a person that is only interested in his success and no one else's. Be considerate, and never forget to thank them for their assistance.

Look for an outlet for frustration.

It is going to happen; you will hit a brick wall. To maintain your sanity, you need an outlet for your frustration. If you are a physical person, take up running or pump iron. If you are a more spiritual person, use prayer or meditation. In some cases, use both. Pent-up frustration will make you say things you do not mean, make critical errors in judgment, or handle matters inappropriately. If you feel frustrated in the presence of others, quietly remove yourself from the situation. When choosing an outlet, find something that will build your body, mind and/or soul. A lot of people choose outlets that have negative outcomes. Do not let that be you.

Falling out can be avoided. We must have the discipline to persist and move past the problem. Be empowered.

Chapter 6:

Use Your Past,
Not Abuse Your Past

IｌｌｌｌｌｌｌＩ

"Too many people overvalue what they are not
and undervalue what they are."

-Malcolm S. Forbes
Former Publisher of Forbes Magazine

The only impediment to success, in many
cases, is ourselves. We look back at the past and
say, "I've gone through so much, no one is going
to want me"; or "I didn't come from a good
family and no one is going to help me"; or "I
have been abused, I am never going to find
someone who will love me"; or "I have lost so
much ground, there is no way I am going to be

successful." These are the statements of an individual who is "abusing his past."

When we abuse our past, we use past events to explain why success is not obtainable. We proclaim failures, setbacks, and life circumstances as the reasons why we cannot achieve the desires of our heart. We may fail at a task once, and from that point forward, say that we are incapable of completing the task. Recognize that the past can be a dynamic tool for the future when used properly.

A past of setbacks, challenges, frustrations, disappointments, failures, and problems can truly be a good thing. Think about it. Your past can serve as a conditioning tool for your future. When I was in high school, I walked everywhere. I walked from home to school, from school to work, and from work to home, carrying my personal items and books. My walking routine served me well in the military. A road march was a twelve-mile march in full combat gear, and I did well, because I was conditioned by my past. When I entered basic training, sleep was limited, and many individuals in my unit were not use to working on limited hours of sleep. However, I could do so because I worked many hours during high school and had no problem dealing with sleep deprivation. Your past can serve to strengthen and develop you.

Research has shown that difficult events in life can have benefits. Drs. Thomas W. Britt, Amy B. Adler, and Paul T. Bartone examined the effects of difficult events on an individuals' development. They found that past stressful events helped individuals cope better with future events or problems. In their article, "Deriving Benefits from Stressful Events: the Role Engagement in Meaningful Work and Hardiness," published in the *Journal of Occupational Health Psychology,* they explain:

> In theoretical terms, hardiness has been defined as a dispositional tendency to find meaning in events,

particularly stressful events that challenge the individual. Past research has suggested that hardy individuals are less likely to exhibit physical symptomatology in the face of high levels of stress, in part because that construes the stress as a challenge that is capable of being mastered. Therefore, it makes theoretical sense that hardiness should be related to deriving benefits from stressful experiences.[1]

The adage "what does not kill you makes you stronger" is scientifically sound. Your difficulties not only help to condition you for the future, but also serve as a testament of your resiliency.

Take a moment and think about the following: If you were able to survive a past chock-full of difficulties and hardships, the future is extremely bright. You were able to survive the tough times and grow because of it. When I look back on my past, I do not see just the hardships, but I see a bright future. I had nowhere to go but up. Instead of saying, "Because I am poor, I can't be what I want to be," I said, "Because I've gone through poverty, I am definitely going to make it." I recognized that my past was not my limitation; it was a part of my destination.

When a person uses his past properly, he realizes that past difficulties are not the end but the beginning. I had many setbacks: my father abandoned me, my family's loss of income, my brother's epilepsy, my conscription into the working poor, and, a real low point, when I ate ice for meals. However, I did what I am sharing with you: I used my past. I said to myself, "If I can survive these hardships, I can beat anything that comes to me." I understood that my past made me tough enough for whatever I would face in the future.

Most people do not think of themselves as tough. They say, "I'm getting slapped around by life." You are tough enough because each day you engage and fight "the good fight." You are tough because you are taking one more step, making one more phone call, going to one more interview, making one more payment, and giving out one more business card. My friend, that is toughness. You could have folded on life.

People fold on life because it is easy. It is easier to say, "I have gone through so much, and I'm done. I don't want to keep going." Your mental toughness is a direct result of the adversities you face. Each trial in your past has prepared you for your future. I know from experience that the adversity I faced prepared me for bigger and better opportunities. You can miss the lessons if you are not paying attention and learning from these experiences.

As I started changing my life for the better, I looked back on my past and smiled. People note that I smile often, and I smile because I appreciate how the Lord has given me the opportunities to elevate myself. I smile because I think about when it rained in my house or when I walked miles and miles to a minimum wage job. I smile because I realize I am blessed and that life is truly a gift. I look at my past and see how good my life has truly become. I am married to a beautiful woman who is the love of my life, and we have three great children. I am able to provide for them in a greater capacity than I would have been able to do in the past. I smile with every victory, because I remember the times of defeat. I am thankful for the hard times, because they helped me appreciate the good times.

Dear friend, I encourage you not to look back at your past for shortcomings, but to look forward to the victories ahead.

End Note:

Britt, Thomas W.; Adler, Amy B.; Bartone, Paul T. "Deriving benefits from stressful events: The role of engagement in meaningful work and hardiness." *Journal of Occupational Health Psychology,* Vol. 6(1), January 2001, p. 53-63.

Lesson 6:

Creating A New Life

We are not victims of our past, for the past may hold the key to the future. If you are trying to create a new life, the tips below will help.

Define your new life.

Define your future in clear and unambiguous terms, because you need to know where you are going. On a sheet of paper, write what you desire for your life, and be as specific as possible. Place the desire for the future on a timeline; this will let you know where you are in the process. Plans are subject to change, so be flexible enough to adjust with the changing tide, but strong enough to not compromise your vision.

Look in the past and see what you can use.

We have experiences, skills, and knowledge that are applicable to our pursuits; all we must do is recognize the connection. For example, an individual who has worked as a cashier in a grocery store would be a prime candidate to work in a bank as a teller or a customer service representative. The skills required are fundamentally the same: count cash and do not come up short on the till. Write down all your skills, jobs, and experiences, and then compare the list against your current desires. Identify the skills and experiences that you can exploit to reach your desired future.

Seek opportunities for advancement.

Opportunities for advancement come in

different forms. Your advancement opportunity may be educational development via formal or self-education, experiential development via involvement with a job or civic organization, or cultural development via attendance of cultural or fine arts events. Opportunities for advancement are everywhere; they can take place at home by watching educational programming on television or listening to it on the radio; curiosity is the key. Community colleges are fantastic sources of personal and professional development and are affordable. A community college is a great place to be retrained in a new field. Find a community college in your area, review the class schedules, and see what interests you.

Dissolve unproductive relationships.

Relationships play a pivotal part in the

development of our life. Destructive relationships hold us back and make it hard to move forward. If a relationship chronically takes an emotional, financial, physical or spiritual toll on you, this is a destructive relationship. A boyfriend or girlfriend who cheats on you, the family member who steals money, or a friend who is being two-faced—these are destructive relationships. Remove these people from your life, as you are better off without them.

Moving toward a new future can be scary, but you are equipped for the challenge. Be empowered.

Chapter 7:

If You Stay Ready, You Don't Have to Get Ready

▌▐▌▐▌

"Practice doesn't make perfect.
Perfect practice makes perfect."

-Vince Lombardi
Football Hall of Fame Coach

One of my favorite mantras, "If you stay ready, you don't have to get ready," came from a good friend and trusted advisor, Mr. Randy Moore. He was my Sergeant Major in the 50th Signal Battalion at Fort Bragg, and today, he is a successful entrepreneur. He is the president and CEO of RLM Communications, which has annual revenues of more than $20 million. I cannot remember the first time I heard the quote, but I know that it has stuck with me for a long time. The saying is based on the idea that we must stand ready for opportunities and never neglect the preparation necessary for success.

Whatever you want to do with your life, prepare for it now. If you want to be the next big singer, athlete, model or author, prepare today for that dream. If you plan on being a music artist, when is the last time you went to the studio? If you plan on being a pro athlete, how much time have you spent in the gym? If you plan on being *America's Next Top Model*, where are your recent headshots? Think about how to prepare for your opportunity, because one day, you might get the chance to showcase your skills.

I often tell my students that "once in a lifetime" opportunities are named appropriately; you may have only one chance to impress a decision maker, and you do not want to be practicing on her. The person may hold the keys to the door you want to go through, so be ready for that opportunity. When you are constantly working on your craft and developing yourself, you are making an investment in the future that you want.

You might say, "I am unemployed and have no funds to invest in my future." You do not need money for this type of investment. Libraries and the Internet make it possible to amass great levels of information for self-development for free. Spending an hour or two in the library weekly will help you reap fantastic gains. You can research better methods of approaching your dreams and learn from the mistakes of others. I conducted a search on a public library database and found more than eighteen hundred books with the words "how to" in the title. You can prepare yourself without incurring great cost, but if you have to pay to develop your skills, do so. It is an investment in your future. We waste a great deal of money on items and activities that will not improve our standard of living or quality of life. An investment in your development and preparation will always pay out for you. You are preparing for your "once in a lifetime" opportunity and want to be ready.

I gained my opportunity to teach in a Tier One University because of the concept I am sharing with you. I had a vision of being a professor in the highest ranking educational institution in my area. I started in the community college system as a continuing education instructor, but if you attended my classes, you would have thought that I was teaching at Harvard University. I prepared and taught my classes as if I were in the Tier One University. I went into my classroom with slides, case studies, examples, executive commentary from business publications, presentation notes, and news videos. I walked into my classroom with everything but the kitchen sink. I practiced all of my lectures for the academic year during the summer break to ensure that my delivery was on point. I edited and reedited my course materials to ensure that I was using the latest information. I understood that if I wanted to be in a Tier One University, I had to work like I was in a Tier One University and eventually I would be. I worked hard for five years and was promoted through the system from community college continuing education instructor to community college curriculum instructor; then to visiting assistant professor at a liberal arts college, then to assistant professor at an historically black college, then to teaching assistant professor at the Tier One University.

When my opportunity with the Tier One University came, I was 100 percent ready. My years of preparation paid off in a big way. I earned the respect of my colleagues and my students because of my work ethic. I also won every teaching award that I was eligible for. I won the SGA Distinguished Professor Award. I was inducted into the Academy of Outstanding Teachers. I won the University Teaching Excellence Award. I won the College of Management Teaching Award. I also won the

Diversity Award, the Assessment Award, and the Ujima Award. I won a couple of other awards that if I stated them here, you would think I am bragging. The point is, my preparation paid off. I knew if I were given the chance to teach in the Tier One University, I would have one shot, and I could not blow it.

Mr. Moore's cogent and well-placed advice is correct. Prepare for your success today, because your opportunity might be right around the corner. Dear friend, stay ready so you do not have to get ready.

Lesson 7:

Planning

Planning is another important aspect of success. Not having a plan is like trying to build a skyscraper without blueprints. The following are tips for developing a life plan.

Know what is important to you.

You are the only person that lives your life. You know your heart's desire more than anyone, with the exception of the Creator. Be clear on what you want out of life. Do not feel what you desire is petty. For example, some authors do not address the fact that their readers need money to live. In turn, the reader feels bad about having money as a goal. Do not apologize for wanting financial resources. You need financial resources to make it in this world. If you are living in a housing project, sleeping on a carpet and wondering if your utilities are going to work, having financial resources may mean something to you. I have two caveats: (1) Do not lust after money; the money becomes your god, and you start making questionable moral and legal decisions. (2) Do not make money the source of your happiness. If you lose the money, you lose your happiness and peace of mind. Having money as a goal is not wrong, but be clear on what is important to you. Not what is important to me or anyone else, but you.

Analyze your resource needs, and devise a plan to obtain the resources.

Executing a plan will take resources, and not just financial resources. Your plan may require the resources of time or credentialing. It also may need the resources of relationship or connections. Identify those resources early, and take a quick inventory. Do you have those resources or need to acquire them? If you have the resources, proceed with the plan. If you do not have the resources, see if there are substitutes. If substitutes are not available, factor in the time that it will take to acquire them. Time horizons are regularly wrong because the factor of resource requirements has not been accounted for; do not let that be you.

Have a back-up plan.

Many times things do not go as planned, so you need a back-up plan to overcome unforeseen problems. A Plan B, C, and in some cases, D will help you to keep moving forward. People have often told me "you can't plan for everything," but it is better to have a plan of some sort than none at all. The "you can't plan for everything" rebuttal is not going to stop the bank from collecting on your mortgage, the utility worker from turning off your lights, or the repo man from repossessing your car. You cannot account for the actions of others and situations outside of your control, but you do have control over your responses to the world. When developing a back-up plan, think about the worst-case scenario and variations of that case. Develop alternative ways to combat the problems. Back-up plans are about being proactive, not reactive. Your back-up plans will keep you mentally aware and give you a sense of confidence.

Schedule relaxation time.

Make sure to leave space for rest and relaxation. Success is a marathon, not a sprint. You are going to need rest to get

to the next level, and you will need your battery recharged. Make sure that rest and relaxation are on your agenda.

In the words of Hannibal from the movie *A-Team,* "I love it when a plan comes together!" Plan your work, and work your plan. Reach your potential. Be empowered.

Chapter 8:

No Excuses

> "The difference between a successful person and others is not a lack of strength, not a lack of knowledge, but rather in a lack of will."
>
> -Vince Lombardi
> Football Hall of Fame Coach

Excuses can become corrosive. An excuse does not get you any closer to reaching your desired goals. People make many excuses for their failure to achieve, such as the following:

"I'm black, and they are never going to hire me."

"I'm a woman and there has never been a female partner at this firm."

"I'm too young."

"I'm too old."

"I'm too short."

"I'm too tall."

It does not matter what the excuse is, it is still an excuse. Do not get into the habit of making excuses. You have more power than you think. When you make excuses, you vacate control over your life. In essence, you are saying that your circumstances and issues are greater than you.

In psychology, the perspective of control over one's life is referred to as the locus of control. This was coined by the personality researcher, Dr. Julian Rotter. The locus of control focuses on whether a person believes he has control over his given circumstances (internal locus of control) or believes that outcomes are beyond his control (external locus of control). When we make excuses, we take the external position of blaming the world for our circumstances; this is not productive. If we want success, we must take the internal view of responsibility for our lives. Making excuses does not change the situation before us. The time wasted on the "blame game" could be spent on finding solutions.

Solutions fix problems, not excuses. I have worked with individuals that made excuses for their lack of productivity. I have heard everything from "the other employees are giving me a hard time because of my background" to "I am not being respected in my role." I had a hard time believing these individuals, because in many cases, they were late for meetings, turned in work late, and missed critical deadlines. These individuals made excuses to blame others for their shortcomings and refused to "face the music" and accept responsibility for their failures. In my opinion, these people seemed to believe that assigning blame to others was the best way to deal with problems. The excuses often destroyed the creditability that they were trying to create. Had they taken responsibility for their shortcomings and committed to fixing the shortcomings, the outcome would have been completely different. Had the individual said, "Hey guys, I messed up. I'm working on this issue, but I need some help," their colleagues could have respected that. Making excuses does not fix the problem, it only makes it worse.

I realize that there are organizations that are sexist, racist, homophobic, anti-Semitic, elitist, inequitable, unreasonable, and the like, but using these as the excuse for inaction is a cop out. Racism is alive and well in America, but if you are a minority, racism should not stop you from being your very best. Sexism is as present in our society today as it was twenty years ago, but if you are woman, sexism should not be your reason for lack of productivity. Those are excuses used to maintain and protect ego. It is easy to say, "I did not get the promotion because I am a woman" (or minority) while neglecting the fact that you did not come to work on time for the last year. It is easy to say, "Because of the good old boys club, I cannot get to the top" while neglecting the fact that you have not done a third of the work of your other colleagues. If you think your failure is attributed to discrimination or inequity, you control where you work and who you share your talents with. Who is in charge of your life—you or the good old boys? If the boys do not want you in their club, build your own.

Making excuses for a lack of achievement is unhealthy and unproductive. Do you remember the story of Cain and Abel? If not, here is a quick refresher. Cain and Abel were brothers; Cain worked the land and Abel tended to the sheep. Cain and Abel both made offerings to the Lord, and when Cain offered a lesser quality offering, his offering was found to be unsatisfactory. Abel offered the first and most desirable of his flock in offering, and his offering was found to be good. Furious with the disposition of his offering and the favor of the Lord toward Abel, Cain killed his brother. Cain is the perfect example of making excuses. Instead of examining the offering he presented, he went right for the excuse. He saw the situation as being his brother's fault.

Be honest—how many times have you looked at another person's accomplishments and said, "I could have done that, if it was not for" or "the only reason they were able to do that was because of?" Instead of examining your part in the situation, you made an excuse to get yourself off the hook. Do not be a Cain.

You are better than those excuses. You are better than being envious of another person's accomplishments. You have the power to affect the outcome—no excuses.

Lesson 8:

How to Avoid Excuses

When we make an excuse, we try to reassign responsibility for failure to someone or something, but if we take steps and follow through, we will not need to make excuses. Below are a few tips to help you develop a "no excuses" life.

Manage time and commitments.

Evaluate and rank your current commitments. Use a calendar and map all your commitments. When you have completed this, evaluate the importance and time requirement of each commitment. If the commitment is not important, eliminate it. Contact the person in charge and explain that you do not have the adequate amount of time to properly address the commitment. If the commitment is important, do not deviate from the path. The old adage of "your word is your bond" should stand true.

Communicate with stakeholders.

The term "stakeholder" refers to individuals or organizations that have an interest in your business activities. We all have stakeholders in life: the individuals that we interact with that may depend upon us. Communicating with the key stakeholders in your life will prevent items from sneaking up on you. When you are surprised, you are more likely to make an excuse. Ask questions of the people you are dealing with; this is an appropriate practice in every facet of your life. In business, speaking with your partners can reduce waste and loss. In marriage, engaging your spouse can prevent confusion and emotional pain. In school, talking with your teacher can avert a poor grade. When communicating with an individual, be sure that you clarify the expectations of the relationship, agree upon standards for performance, and reiterate the desired goals. You will not have to later make excuses, because you will be informed and know the expectations.

Think ahead.

Thinking of a problem before it occurs minimizes the likelihood of it ever occurring. In your work, think about some of the problems that may occur relating to your job, and then construct a plan to deal with the problem. This is a good way to deal with problems because you have the benefit of time and information. In the throes of a problem, you may not have time to think or you may think through the problem half-way, which can result in a poor outcome. When dealing with an issue on the spot, you may not have the opportunity to seek counsel. However, when you think ahead, you can get all the advice you need. In my PhD program, I saw a problem with the low graduation rate. I decided to consult several upper classmen and ask why they had difficulties graduating. Armed with this information, I developed a plan to address the problems that had plagued my colleagues. I was able to research the university's rules and procedures without the pressure of a looming deadline. Thinking ahead can save you time, money, and stress.

Operate with integrity.

I must admit, I am a "Law & Order" junkie; they got me hooked. When I hear the "dun dun" sound of the intro, I run for the couch. During the course of the show, the detectives investigating a crime question witnesses and follow leads to give the district attorney a solid case, and then the DA prosecutes the offender. Within an hour, an entire case is solved from investigation to prosecution, and I am a happy camper. There is a good lesson about integrity in this television show. Sometimes, the detectives have to "strong arm" a witness to speak up. They use threats from calling the IRS to telling a spouse of an extramarital affair. The person complies with the detectives to avoid certain ruin; this is the point of operating with integrity. When you operate with integrity, you do not have to fear anyone or make any excuses. Living your life above board prevents anyone from being able to threaten or intimidate you. When you operate with integrity and attend to your responsibilities, you do not have to constantly look over your shoulder or wonder when you are going to be found out. When you operate with integrity, you do not have to worry about hearing the "dun dun" sound in your life.

Living a "no excuses life" starts with the first step of taking responsibility for your life. Be empowered.

Chapter 9:

Something New Comes In, Something Old Goes Out

│▐│▌│

"The chains of habit are generally too small to be felt until they are too strong to be broken."

-Samuel Johnson
English Author

Fr something new to come into your life, something old must go out. To obtain something better for your life, you must leave old ways behind. Success is predicated on the concept of change and adaptation, and you must change to reach higher levels of success and, in some cases, learn new habits. If you want to lose weight, you have to relinquish overeating, lack of exercise, and poor diet choices. You have to introduce a regimen of exercise and disciplined eating. You must let go of some things and allow entrance to others, and this creates balance.

We are granted only twenty-four hours in a day; the amount of time we can devote to things that are important is limited. We have finite amounts of energy, attention, and focus to devote to the activities of our lives, so we must be good stewards of the resources that we have been granted. To receive the new things in our lives, let go of the old. For example, a person who wants to improve in school but is currently achieving low grades must reallocate his time. He will have to devote more time and energy to his studies. The time he needs must come from somewhere, so he may have to stop staying out late or hanging out with his friends. It comes down to a basic question: Do you want a better life?

The question of a better life was illustrated to me through a conversation with a fortune teller. I had a fortune teller "read" my future. He used a deck of tarot cards and started laying them out on the table. He completed the card formation and said, "You have an extremely bright future. I have never seen a person with so many favorable cards in one reading." Curiosity got the better of me, and I asked, "What if my cards have been all negative, then what?" The gentlemen replied, "Think of the cards as a barometer. If you stay on your path, you will reach the end stated in the cards. However, you can wake up tomorrow, decide to go in another direction, and you will change your future." The message was valuable. If you want a different outcome, you are going to have to go a different way. Do you want a better life than what you currently have? If so, you may have to change your actions to reach that end. If not, maintain your current course and you will reach that end. In many cases, change is required to reach success; you will stop one pursuit and start another. The power of stopping is important in this process.

The power to stop engaging in a certain activity is just as important as the introduction of something new. In my consultation practice, I am often asked, "What do I need to do with this problem?" "What actions should I take?" "What should I add?" In many cases, the problem is not addition but subtraction. The client needs to stop engaging in unprofitable and unproductive practices. People can be so action oriented that they forget that some situations can be improved by simply stopping. For example, a woman struggling with self-esteem can be assisted when she stops associating with people who are intentionally cruel to her. For "addition" to take place, she must "subtract" negative people from her life. She will not reach her highest potential by merely adding things on top of the negative, and if she does not remove those individuals from her life, they will undo the positive with their negative attitudes.

Dear friend, for something new to come into your life, something old must go. You are the steward of your resources, and how you allocate those resources will determine your success.

Lesson 9:

Arranging Life

Life is a continual process of change. The following tips will help you ensure that the changes are what you want.

Take inventory of your life.

Take a sheet of paper, and draw a line down the middle. On one side, list the good and on the other list the bad things affecting your life. Transfer the items from the "good" column to another sheet of paper, and place it on your bathroom mirror. Every morning, review those good items in your life and be thankful for them. This is a great way to start the day. Construct a plan to remove the items from the "bad" column. For example, if a volatile relationship is ruining your life, commit to eliminating this relationship. I remember an old blues song, "I Can Do Bad by Myself." The title illustrates the point that you can do badly alone, so remove the relationships that hinder your progress.

Seek resources.

There are thousands of organizations in the United States focused on assisting individuals. You can find help for everything from starting a business to battling addiction. The key is finding organizations that can assist you and properly using the resources. Start with the library. Many librarians are trained in accessing databases and research methodologies, and the library may sponsor community activities that can be of assistance. Once you have found the organization or informational resource, act. A common misconception is that "information is power." The *application* of information is power, which is knowledge.

Monitor progress.

Take the time to review your progress. You can track the distance between your current position and your desired destination, which will help with motivation. As you move forward, each victory will inspire you. Do not compare your progress with someone else's. For example, do not say, "Jack made it to management by age twenty-eight, and I am already twenty-eight. I'm behind." This only serves to frustrate you and may make you feel like you have not accomplished enough. Compare yourself only with yourself, and appreciate the distance that you have traveled.

Change presents new opportunities and challenges, but you are up to the task. Be empowered.

Chapter 10:
Play to Win

"Don't sit down and wait for the opportunities to come. You have to get up and make them for yourself."

-Madame C.J. Walker
Businesswoman

"Play to win" sounds simplistic, but there is a lot to discuss on this point. Many people are not playing the game of life to win; they are trying to maintain a low-loss record. There is an inherent difference. When a person plays to win, he does not mind making mistakes, facing setbacks, or confronting fear. He understands that adversity is par for the course and as natural as breathing. However, the person attempting to maintain a low-loss record does not engage challenges, flee situations where failure is possible, or limit activities to areas where victory is guaranteed. Playing to win is proactive, while low loss is reactive.

I saw the phenomena of low loss in the university environment. I noticed that I had several students that were primarily focused on maintaining or obtaining a 4.0 grade point average, and these students obsessed over their GPA. Sometimes their focus on GPA got in the way of learning, because they did only things that maintained or increased their GPA to the detriment of learning. The students held on dearly to their GPA because it was something they had been successful with and thought it was safe. Many were not involved in extracurricular activities that would have improved their learning or future career prospects. I began each semester explaining that a 4.0 GPA alone would not guarantee employment or admission into graduate school. Many of them were habitual overachievers and had never known failure; sadly, some of them had a difficult time gaining employment when they completed their studies. What happened?

In a good number of cases, the 4.0 GPA students were trying to maintain a low-loss record and missed critical opportunities for growth and development. Meanwhile, their colleagues with lower GPAs successfully entered the job market. The lower-GPA students tried new things and were not scared of failing at a task. This provided the students with a stronger resume and experience to talk about during interviews. This example crystallizes an important insight about a low-loss mentality. The person with the low-loss mentality says, "I made no mistakes, I got it right the first time, I never lost" but misses an important part in the analysis: he did not win either. Just because you did not lose does not mean you won.

In the military, I worked with a gentleman named "Bob" who was extremely intelligent and talented, but he did not play to win. In my opinion, he played to maintain a low-loss record and did not challenge himself. I encouraged him to take college classes with me, but he rarely went; I encouraged him to do physical training with me, but he did not train. He had been passed over for promotion numerous times and other less talented individuals were promoted over him, but he had no one to be mad at but himself. In my opinion, he did not stretch himself. He was focused on not losing, but he did not win. He stayed in his comfort zone and did not give the board a reason to promote him. He did only what was comfortable.

Being uncomfortable makes you stronger. When you go to the gym, if you do not lift heavier weights, you are never going to get stronger. Playing to win exposes you to challenges that make you stronger and better. In Bob's case, he only did things that he had mastered and never got out of his comfort zone. Playing to win would have been the difference in Bob's career, but he played to maintain a low-loss record and set himself up for failure in the long run.

In interactions with our bosses, we can play to win. A lot of people are scared of their bosses, because they do not know what their bosses are going to say to them. When their boss comes down the hallway, they run down another hall to avoid having an uncomfortable conversation. Have those conversations with your boss. Find out what he wants and needs. It is better to play offense than wait for him to tell you what you are doing wrong. Find out from your boss what is going wrong and then correct those things. If you do not want to do what your boss wants you to, or you feel uncomfortable doing them, find another boss. Get another job. It is better that you take control.

Many of us are stressed, have heart attacks, suffer from hypertension, battle migraines, and are in dire need of rest because we give too much control to others. When your boss and your circumstances control you, it causes unnecessary stress. You may be scared that one day your boss will come to you and say,

"You're fired," "Here's this pink slip," "I didn't like your performance," or "We don't need you any longer." Instead of waiting for the hammer to fall, play to win, and take the initiative to discover what is needed.

Playing to win gives you control because you direct your path. No one else is dictating your position and direction. You are saying, "This is the path I choose. If you don't like that path, that is fine, as you do not have to go on this journey with me." When you play to win, control is in your hands.

Dear friend, I encourage you to play to win, because it can make all the difference in the outcome of the game.

Lesson 10:

Achieving Results

The goal of playing to win is to achieve a desired result, and reaching results does not occur by accident. The tips below will help you achieve the results you are looking for.

Set SMART goals.

SMART stands for Specific, Measurable, Attainable, Relevant, and Time bounded. Reaching a given goal is about being clear on the direction that you are heading. As you start to engage a goal, write a clear goal statement. This statement will guide your actions and give purpose to your activities. It will also make it harder for you to get distracted and deviate from your purpose.

Seek counsel.

When you are trying to accomplish something new, seek counsel from someone who is experienced in the area. You may be able to find this person by attending conferences or local gatherings or asking people in your network. When you find that person, make sure not only to ask about his successes but also about his setbacks. Failure can be an instructive process. Learning from the failures of others will help you to avoid critical mistakes. Make sure you thank the person, and keep him posted on your progress.

Execute the plan.

Once you have formulated the plan, execute it. Execution is critical in success. You can have the best plan in the world, but if you fail to execute it, it is like having no plan at all. I have seen great plans die in the execution stage, but I have seen mediocre plans that were well executed and a success. Execution is about discipline. You can improve your discipline by asking yourself, "What is mission critical for today?" I learned about this question in the military. "Mission critical" applies to what is absolutely necessary for continued operation. Once you have identified the mission-critical tasks of your day, make sure those are accomplished. Schedule at least one hour of your work day when you cannot be interrupted; this time should be devoted to the completion of mission-critical tasks. During this time, you should not be multitasking. If you have to start your day an hour earlier, do so. The only way your plan will be executed is with undivided attention.

Learn from setbacks and successes.

Learning is a fundamental part of development, and the same is true for getting results. The value of our experience is only useful when we reflect and use the knowledge obtained through the experience in the future. As you reach results, you will face setbacks, and that is okay, because setbacks are part of the process. The key is to learn from the setbacks to improve future prospects. Learning from success is also valuable. After you have executed a plan, review what did or did not go well. Eliminate the practices that did not go well and replicate the things that worked. This will help you to avoid future mistakes and enhance current activities.

Your plan, execution, and learning are all factors in the type of results you will get. Be empowered.

Chapter 11:

You are Your Associations

You have probably heard one of these maxims, "Birds of a feather flock together" or "If you hang out with the wolves, you will start to howl." These adages encapsulate the importance of the company that you keep. Our friends, associates, colleagues, and others influence our levels of success. The people we interact with help to shape our thoughts, values, beliefs, and sometimes life directions; this is why it is so important to monitor the type of people we let into our lives. The people we associate with can be an impediment or impetus to our success.

Think about it. If you spend your time with people who are not going anywhere, how long will it be before you assume their perspectives and thoughts as your own? How long before your motivation starts to lag? How long before you make statements like "It's hopeless," "I don't know why I even tried," or "I can't make it?" How long before you become as depressed as the negative individuals you are associating with? The answer is, "Not very long."

When you associate with people who are positive and trying to achieve something in life, your stock goes up. You will be positively influenced by the person. How long before you start saying, "If they made it, I can make it too," or "I have the skills for that," or "This isn't so tough?" Your associations rub off on you easily; this is why it is imperative to mind the company you keep. Keep the right company, and life opens up with new opportunities.

I have been truly blessed to have associated with some dynamic people. I have met and befriended many senior executives in Fortune 500 companies and top-ranking government officials. I have had the pleasure of working with some of the most amazing people, from bright intellectuals to superb leaders. I try my best to associate with people who are positive, focused, and have the desire to achieve. The people I chose to associate with were not just people with a lot of money in their bank accounts, but people who have a passion for life. They were people who wanted to be good students, were striving for excellence in their parental roles, desired to be pillars of their communities, or were generally interested in living a fulfilled life. I recognized early that if I associated with people who were "going somewhere" and demonstrated good life habits, I would be fortunate if some of their habits rubbed off on me. Their habits did.

I adopted the mentalities and habits of some fantastic people, which help to shape my success. This is why I know the truth of this concept, because I have seen it first-hand. For example, my good friend, Mr. Randy Moore, is a perfect illustration. Randy is many years my senior, but you cannot tell when we get together. His excitement about the entrepreneurial process is outstanding. I learned from him the importance of being positive about entrepreneurship even in the face of insurmountable odds. After I see Randy, I am excited and want to launch more companies. He often tells me that the feeling is mutual and welcomed. Our friendship is not only about business but about encouragement and shared successes among friends.

Another example is my good friend, Dr. Frank Godfrey. Frank is in his sixties but is as active and as sharp as anyone you would ever meet. He is an intellectual dynamo with three degrees from Harvard University. From Frank, I learned the importance of storytelling, a skill that I am often praised for. Frank encouraged me through his example in the classroom, and to this day, I ask for his advice when confronted with an instructional problem that I cannot solve. I look at Frank not only as a mentor but as a father figure.

I have yet another example, my good friend, Mr. Thomas Easley. Thomas and I are the same age, born in the same month (ten days apart) and from the same home state. When I meet with Thomas, ideas flow. Thomas is an individual of many different skills and talents. He is like a superhero; by day, a well-respected university administrator, by night, a hip hop artist that can rock the house. I learned from him the importance of following your dreams no matter how far away they are. These examples help demonstrate the importance of the company you keep. Each of your associations brings a different energy to your life and ultimately to your success.

I hate to go Zen on you, but follow me on this. Our life is no more than the energies influenced upon it. In other words, positive energy equals positive results, and negative energy equals negative results. Each person we choose to associate with has energy to them. We may know this energy by other terms such as *attitude, disposition, personality, persona*, and so on. The name of the energy is not as important as the essence of the characterization. To maintain a forward and upward trajectory in life, you must surround yourself with positive and uplifting people. In the words of Chazz Palminteri's character, Sonny, from the film *A Bronx's Tale,* "Trouble's like a cancer. You got to get it early. You don't get it early, it gets too big, and then it kills you." In the same vein, negative people are a cancer that you must catch early and eliminate, if you want your success to live. Oh by the way, you should not be a cancer to anyone else.

A core value in the medical field is "First, do no harm." This concept can be applied to broader categories, particularly in the area of our associations. There are times I want to get on a rant about something bad, but I have to stop myself and ask, "Is this the energy this person needs to get through his day?" or "Is this the message that I was sent here to deliver?" The answer is "no." I am not talking about wearing blinders to issues that arise—accountability is important—but I am referring to honing on about negative circumstances without action or attempting to derail another person's peace. We have a responsibility to mind the mental disposition and internal working of others. In other words, because you are having a bad day does not give you the right to destroy another person's day. Just because you have experienced a failure does not give you the right to rain on another person's parade. Your success will be secured if you learn to "first do no harm" in your associations.

If you associate with positive, inspiring people, you are one step closer to becoming a positive and inspiring person. Dear friend, I encourage to you to remember that you are your associations.

Lesson 11:

Developing Relationships

Relationships are vital to success in life. The relationships we forge and grow can help us to reach higher levels in our quality of life and standard of living. The following tips will help you develop and manage relationships.

Search for opportunities to engage.

No matter how smart or skilled a person is, if no one knows, it will not help him to move forward. Do you think that Jessica Simpson is the best singer in America? This is a matter of opinion, but the point is that she is the most well-known. Through her relationships with record labels and the media, she has maintained a seat in popular culture. You may not be interested in becoming a pop star, but the rules are the same. Get involved in your industry, and look for opportunities to showcase your skills. Whatever you want to do, there is a professional organization that represents the interests of the profession, and opportunities to become engaged are plentiful. The adage "it is not what you know but who you know" rings true. More opportunities are available for individuals that engage and participate in the process. Go to the Internet and look for opportunities to get engaged. The opportunity that you want may be right around the corner.

Follow up with people.

After attending an event, make follow-up contacts whenever possible. Send an email or leave a voicemail; if you really want to leave an impression, send a handwritten note to the person's office. Remember one fact about the individual, and write the fact on the back of his business card. After the initial follow-up, check in with him the next week. This is how relationships are built, with time and consideration.

Get a mentor.

A mentor can help guide you through your development process, can help to open doors for you, and will advise you as you proceed with your plan of action. The mentor relationship is not to be taken lightly. Selection of a mentor is very important to the success of the relationship, so choose wisely. Before asking a person to be your mentor, do your homework. Find out all you can about him to ensure that you are compatible. That is not to say your mentor must be your same race, gender, or religion. Your mentor can come from a different demographic or background and be valuable to your development. You can have many different mentors, and they will develop into a council of trusted advisors.

Under-promise and over-deliver.

People know you by your habits and characteristics. If you constantly run late for meetings, you will become known as *unreliable*. On the other hand, if you are person who delivers what you promised and more, you will become known as *dependable, reliable,* and most important, *trustworthy*. Do not promise something that you cannot deliver. It is okay to say, "I will not be able to do this," because it is better to say "no" than to not deliver at all. You manage the way the world sees you by way of your actions.

Say thank you.

What your mother told you is true. *Please* and *thank you* take you a long way. Thank the people who have helped you, as that "thank you" today could open a door tomorrow. Being considerate can only help you toward success. Success is not achieved purely through the efforts of one person but through a network of individuals. Thank those who help you, and you will never regret you did.

Check in periodically.

Calling someone out of the blue may brighten their day. Check in with your people "just to say hi." If you call people only when you need something, eventually they will stop returning your calls.

Relationships are delicate items. It may take years to build a relationship but only minutes to destroy it. Guard your relationships like you guard your reputation, and you will prosper. Be empowered.

Chapter 12:

Presentation Counts

"Our work is the presentation of our capabilities."

-Edward Gibbon
Historian

You know the old adage, "Don't judge a book by its cover." It is a fantastic piece of advice that many people do not follow. It is unfortunate that we live in a society that sometimes holds style in higher regard than substance. Individuals who could contribute to the growth of our communities, businesses and lives may be disfranchised because of their appearance. Though we are all guilty of making snap judgments about a person because of his appearance, or speech, it is crucial to understand that your success is dependent upon your presentation. Think about it. The first time we meet a person, sometimes his personal presentation is the only information we have to assess his character. Everything counts, from the clothes he is wearing to the handshake he offers; from the first words he utters to the manners he displays. An evaluation is occurring from the moment we meet. I am not condoning judging by outward appearance, but I recognize its presence and influence on the success process. Do not take my word for it; science supports the above statements.

A study conducted by Professors David Carr, Thomas Davies, and Angeline Lavin concluded that appearance influenced student perception about the quality of their professors. In their article, "The Effect of Business Faculty Attire on Student Perceptions of the Quality of Instruction and Program Quality," published in *College Student Journal*, the researchers stated:

It is apparent that the professional appearance and attire of the professor has positive impact on the student's perceptions of a number of traits that are often considered in the evaluation of an academician...It has been documented that attire has communicative power and the nonverbal messages may be much more powerful than the spoken word.[1]

This study makes a strong argument for being a good steward of your personal appearance and presentation. Even in a profession where intellectual prowess is held in the highest regard, personal appearance and presentation have an effect.

You may say, "That makes sense, so do I have to go buy a new Armani wardrobe to be successful?" The answer is "no." It is not the clothes that make the man but the man that makes the clothes. When I got started in the professional world, I was broke. I was that joke, "I was so poor, I couldn't pay attention." An expensive wardrobe was far out of my reach, but I knew that presentation counted, so I went to the local Salvation Army and looked through the racks to find suits that looked up to date. Some of the suits did not fit, so I took them to a tailor and had the suits fitted for me. I purchased a couple of white and light blue shirts. With the addition of a few ties and well-shined shoes, the look was complete. I was ready to go take on the world.

People assumed that I was wearing the latest Brooks Brothers or Armani, but I was wearing the latest Salvation Army. I knew instinctively that it was not the clothes but how I wore them. My appearance and presence was the key, not a label or brand. I could have been wearing Tommy Hilfiger, but if I did not pay attention to how I carried myself, it would not matter. Some people misconstrue "presentation counts" to mean that you must have the latest fashion or spend hundreds of dollars to obtain fine clothing. This is definitely not what I am saying; I am suggesting focusing on how you present yourself.

You can be poor but make a better presentation than a person with millions of dollars in the bank. Let us refer back to the Salvation Army example; I beat out a lot of individuals who had more financial resources. I focused intently on making sure that I had the right content and that I presented myself well. My suits were pressed better, my shoes were shinier, and my ties were tied better. When I opened my mouth, I made sure I had something to say and that my statements were based on facts or well-thought-out reasoning.

I also want to make a clear statement about content. No matter how good a presentation, eventually content will be brought into question. Make sure whenever you make a presentation, your content is 100 percent together. In our age of bells and whistles, it is easy to forget about content, but it can be a difference maker. Your presentation is not limited to your physical attributes but is also accounted for in your work.

When your boss, teacher, parent, or leader assigns you a project, he may not say, "Make it look good and organized," but he will not decline these qualities in your work. This is going the extra mile. The next time you are asked to do work for someone, make the final product nicer, more organized, clearer, or better formatted. You will be surprised by the response. My colleagues in the university and other organizations marveled at the depth, completeness, and beauty of my work. It eventually became my hallmark. They said, "Give it to David, because it will get done and look right." The only reason I gained that reputation was because I made sure that the content was solid and the final product was aesthetically pleasing. My focus on "content first, presentation next" opened many doors. Do not just complete a project; make a statement through your work.

Dear friend, in life, there are extra points

for presentation, so make sure that you get them. Do not forget that presentation counts.

End Note:

Carr, David., Davies, Thomas., and Lavin, Angeline. "The Impact of Instructor Attire on College Student Satisfaction." *College Student Journal* Vol. 44, No. 1, 2010.

Lesson 12:

Making the Presentation

Delivering an effective presentation can be mastered. Here are some tips for making the best presentation possible.

Dress for success.

Look the part. As stated earlier, your physical appearance is where evaluation starts. Your dress should be professional and "well put together." If you do not know what proper business dress is, review a department store catalog. The catalog will have models that are dressed in business attire. Copy the styles as you learn how to coordinate outfits for yourself.

Check your room and equipment.

Murphy's Law is alive and well; everything that can go wrong, will go wrong. Check your equipment. Make sure everything is working, and do a dry run. Arrive early enough to correct any problems that may occur. Inspect your room and make sure that everything is in order before you begin. If you need to move furniture or other items to make the room more conducive for your presentation, do it.

Know your audience.

Knowing your audience plays a critical role in the development and delivery of a presentation. Obtain as much information as possible about the group. Find out the demographic information and the professions of the group members. In this way, you can tailor your presentation and avoid using information that is not relevant to the group. In the words of the wise and great philosopher, G.I. Joe, "Knowing is half the battle."

Be concise.

We have all sat through a presentation that has gone on too long. You will lose your audience, and the audience may not even remember the content you presented. Be thorough but concise; explain the concept using as few words as possible. You will find that less is more. If you use visual aid software such as PowerPoint, do not load the slides with a large amount of text; use graphics, tables, and charts as much as possible. A picture is worth a thousand words.

Keep it simple.

Do not complicate the information. Your audience will appreciate a straightforward, easy-to-understand presentation. Do not let your ego get the better of you. At the podium, you may be tempted to show you are the smartest person in the room; fight this urge. You do not need to prove that you are smart, and people will know when you are trying to "show off." Keep your presentation simple and direct.

Practice, practice, practice.

How do you get to Carnegie Hall? Practice, practice, practice. Practice your presentation multiple times until you feel comfortable with it. Practice will help with nervousness and self-doubt. If your visual aids fail, you will be fine, because you have practiced. Do not memorize your presentation, because if you forget one word, you can miss the entire speech. Be familiar enough with your content that you do not have to memorize.

Tell a story.

A good story can captivate an audience and illustrate a point. People remember stories, because stories tap into the human experience. This is why a comedian can get an audience to roar with laughter because he has touched the core of the listeners. He finds a common thread of human experiences and relates that experience with humor. You do not have to be a comedian, but tell a story that helps the audience to relate to you.

Be excited.

Your audience will only be as excited as you are. If you not fired up about the topic, the audience will not be either. The audience is following you on this journey, and you set the tone. Set a positive, upbeat tone; your audience is depending on it.

Presentation skills can propel you forward or hold you back. Develop this skill to the best of your abilities. Be empowered.

Chapter 13:

Trouble is Easy to Get Into, But Hard to Get Out Of

"It is not falling in the water that makes you drown. It is what you do once you're in there."

-Anonymous

As a young man, I learned an invaluable lesson (one of many) from a distinguished, intelligent, woman, Ms. Clementine Washington, better known as *Mom*. My mother taught me that "Trouble is easy to get into, but hard to get out of." My mother told me and my brother this phrase to remind us how easy it is to lose everything you have worked for with a few brief moments of indiscretion. Before I unpack this concept, first let me tell you about my mother.

My mother is not an extremely educated person, but she gave me an education that would rival any higher education institution. She is not a rich person, but she gave me an inheritance of knowledge that helped me succeed. She was not a leader of an organization, but she taught me that leading others is a privilege and leadership is a responsibility that should not be taken lightly, because, as she said, "People are depending on you, son." I often say in public, "If I could be half the teacher my mother is, I might do something valuable in this world." I am glad that I took many of my mother's lessons to heart. Mom, I love you. Thank you for everything you have done for me. Now, let's move on to the lesson.

Out of anger, frustration, desperation, emotional weakness, loneliness, distress, or fear, we can make decisions that can have negative, long-lasting effects on our lives. We create trouble as a result of poor decision making, or we make a decision in a moment of emotional instability. On the verge of losing your home, you might decide that robbing a bank is not such a bad idea. When you are traveling and meet a person who is so engaging and exciting, and before you know it she is in the hotel room with you, but you are married—trouble. If you are not vigilant, trouble will creep into your life, take everything you have worked for, and leave you emotionally, physically and financially wounded.

Do you remember the Pacers-Pistons basketball brawl of 2004? On November 19, 2004 in Auburn Hills, Michigan, the Detroit Pistons were playing the Indiana Pacers. During the game, the teams became involved in a brawl on the court. The fight moved from the court to the stands when a fan, John Green, threw his drink on Pacers player Ron Artest. Artest entered the seating area to pursue the individual that he thought was responsible for throwing the drink, but he engaged the wrong person in the middle of the skirmish. Other players entered the stands and the fight turned into a mini-riot. The game was televised, and the whole world saw the event. Many of the players were suspended, lost a significant amount of their salary, and faced criminal charges. The fans involved in the brawl faced criminal charges as well. Artest took a beating in the media and his wallet, no pun intended. As a result of the brawl, Artest had to pay over $4 million and he received the longest suspension of all the players. The fight was easy enough to get into, but it created a situation that was extremely hard to get out of.

You may be saying, "What was he supposed to do? Let a person throw a drink on him and walk away?" Absolutely not. If someone attacks you, you have the right to defend yourself, but Artest forgot his surroundings and who he was. As an NBA player, he was not going to be held to the same standard of conduct as a regular person. Is this fair? No, but that is life. I understand that hindsight is always 20/20. It is easy for me to say, sitting in front of a laptop, "He should have done this," or "He should have done that." I use the brawl to illustrate an important point; in life, sometimes there is no dress rehearsal. Irrespective if you think Artest was justified in rushing the stands or not, the fact is that he had to deal with the repercussions. We all are held accountable for our actions. Justified or not, we have to account for every bad decision we make. In Artest's case, he lost critical playing time and financial prosperity. What should he have done? I will not speculate, because that is unfair to Mr. Artest. I will say that we must think thirty seconds beyond the moment we are in.

Once you start down a path, think about the ramifications of your actions, because regardless of right or wrong, you are going to be held accountable. Success in life is based upon the decisions that we make. When we make good decisions, good manifests, but when we make bad decisions, the reverse is true. Therefore, I encourage you to remember my mom's advice, "Trouble is easy to get into, but hard to get out of."

Lesson 13:

Manage Conflicts

Success does not mean that you will not have problems, but successful people learn how to manage conflict. Here are some tips to help you better manage conflict.

Do not say or do the first thing that comes to mind.

In the midst of problems, we often say or do things that we later regret. Our response is based on emotion, not rational thought. This is why it is important to pause before responding to an event. Delaying a response by as few as fifteen seconds could prevent a catastrophe. Think before you act.

When angry, regroup.

When a situation has made you angry,

that is not the best time to try to resolve a problem. If you are angry to the point of yelling, discontinue the conversation for the time being. Tell the person that you would like to revisit the issue at a later time that day or you would like to research the problem and will be back in touch with them to discuss it. Make sure to schedule a time to reconvene, because you do not want to get into the habit of avoidance. By scheduling a time, the person knows that you are committed to resolving the problem.

Speak in terms of behaviors.

In conflict, be specific and clear on the problem. When you are addressing an issue with someone, speak in terms of behavior. Dr. Martin Luther King, Jr. said, "Behavior can be regulated." His point is well taken when dealing with conflict. It is hard to adjust attitude or personal preferences, but behavior can be easily addressed. For example, if someone is speaking to you in a foul manner, let him know that his behavior is unacceptable. Be specific about the behavior and use facts. The more specific you can be about the description of the problem behavior, the better the intervention to combat the behavior. Be brief in your assessment. If you cannot accurately describe the problem behavior in a few moments, commit it to paper. Revise the statement into a few sentences, and practice the delivery style you will use to inform the person. I know this seems like a lot of work, but your preparation can help alleviate problems on the back end.

When wrong, apologize without excuses.

When you are wrong in a situation, apologize without excuses. I have known individuals who seemed physically incapable of offering an apology, or if they did offer an apology, it was a "backhanded apology" accompanied by excuses. You do not win points with people when you do this and you may be seen as an arrogant person who cannot recognize his own faults. When I get into a conflict with someone, I ask myself, "What have I contributed to this situation to cause this problem?" If I did something that was out of order, I immediately seek out the person to offer a heartfelt apology without any excuses. The statement goes like this: "I am sorry for what I did; please forgive me."

Conflicts are a part of life and should be managed, not avoided. Be empowered.

Epilogue

Dear friend, thank you for sharing this portion of your journey with me. I hope that this reading has educated your mind, encouraged your soul, and entertained your imagination. Writing it has provided me with joy, and I hope that my joy and excitement shined through to you. I want to leave you this thought; life is a choice but also a gift.

God has provided you with this precious gift called life, and you only have one. It is up to you to determine what you will do with this valuable gift. I encourage you to look at life as the great opportunity it is and live your life to the fullest. It is with a full heart that I write "be empowered," because the power over your life resides within you. May God bless and keep you and your family. I wish you the best and please, take care of yourself.

Did you like this book?

If you liked this book,
please go to Amazon.com and
post your comments.

About the Author

At 14 years of age, Dr. David Washington's family lost their sole source of income: his mother's low wage job. His family was in danger of being evicted from their modest home and falling deeper into poverty. He made a choice and decided to obtain employment. He knew there had to be something he could do to help his family. He traded his childhood playtime for life lessons in faith, determination, humility and hard work. By the time he was a senior in high school, he was working four jobs, attending school and taking the lion's share of the household responsibilities. The matters were further complicated by his brother's epilepsy. However, he did not take the time to feel sorry for himself; because he innately understood one thing: he had power over his situation.

Dr. Washington took charge and joined the United States Army and worked on his education at night. He completed his bachelor degree in business. Upon completion of his military service, he went back into the world of work and continued pursuing his education at night. He completed two master degrees within 18 months from two different universities. Earning his Master of Business Administration and Master of Science in Administration, he then decided to pursue a doctorate degree from North Carolina State University. Dr. Washington completed his PhD in the record time of three years.

Dr. David Washington is president of Washington & Company, a business consultancy and training company. He has been published in the Leadership and Organizational Management Journal, Franklin Business Law Journal, and the Ethics and Critical Thinking Journal. He has worked with various organizations providing leadership development training. His passion is to educate, encourage and entertain people to reach their full potential.

Index

Made in the USA
Charleston, SC
09 July 2012